成也萧何，败也萧何

Xiao He: A Blessing and a Curse

叶婵娟 改编　吴爱俊 翻译

150 **words**
Starter

First Edition   2018

ISBN 978-7-5138-1479-9
Copyright 2018 by Sinolingua Co., Ltd
Published by Sinolingua Co., Ltd
24 Baiwanzhuang Road, Beijing 100037, China
Tel: (86) 10-68320585 68997826
Fax: (86) 10-68997826 68326333
http://www.sinolingua.com.cn
E-mail: hyjx@sinolingua.com.cn
Facebook: www.facebook.com/sinolingua
Printed by Beijing Jinghua Hucais Printing Co., Ltd

Printed in the People's Republic of China

编者的话

对于广大汉语学习者来说，要想快速提高汉语水平，扩大阅读量是很有必要的。"彩虹桥"汉语分级读物为汉语学习者提供了一系列有趣、有用的汉语阅读材料。本系列读物按照词汇量进行分级，力求用限定的词汇讲述精彩的故事。本套读物主要有以下特点：

一、**分级精准，循序渐进**。我们参考"新汉语水平考试（HSK）词汇表"（2012年修订版）、《汉语国际教育用音节汉字词汇等级划分（国家标准）》和《常用汉语1500高频词语表》等词汇分级标准，结合《欧洲语言教学与评估框架性共同标准》（CEFR），设计了一套适合汉语学习者的"彩虹桥"词汇分级标准。本系列读物分为7个级别（入门级*、1级、2级、3级、4级、5级、6级），供不同水平的汉语学习者选择，每个级别故事的生词数量不超过本级别对应词汇量的20%。随着级别的升高，故事的篇幅逐渐加长。本系列读物与HSK、CEFR的对应级别，各级词汇量以及每本书的字数详见下表。

---

* 入门级（Starter）在封底用S标识。

级别	入门级	1级	2级	3级	4级	5级	6级
对应级别	HSK1 CEFR A1	HSK1-2 CEFR A1-A2	HSK2-3 CEFR A2-B1	HSK3 CEFR A2-B1	HSK3-4 CEFR B1	HSK4 CEFR B1-B2	HSK5 CEFR B2-C1
词汇量	150	300	500	750	1 000	1 500	2 500
字数	1 000	2 500	5 000	7 500	10 000	15 000	25 000

二、故事精彩，题材多样。本套读物选材的标准就是"精彩"，所选的故事要么曲折离奇，要么感人至深，对读者构成奇妙的吸引力。选题广泛取材于中国的神话传说、民间故事、文学名著、名人传记和历史故事等，让汉语学习者在阅读中潜移默化地了解中国的文化和历史。

三、结构合理，实用性强。"彩虹桥"系列读物的每一本书中，除了中文故事正文之外，都配有主要人物的中英文介绍、生词英文注释及例句、故事正文的英文翻译、练习题和生词表，方便读者阅读和理解故事内容，提升汉语阅读能力。练习题主要采用客观题，题型多样，难度适中，并附有参考答案，既可供汉语教师在课堂上教学使用，又可供汉语学习者进行自我水平检测。

如果您对本系列读物有什么想法，比如推荐精彩故事、提出改进意见等，请发邮件到 liuxiaolin@sinolingua.com.cn，与我们交流探讨。也可以关注我们的微信公众号 CHQRainbowBridge，随时与我们交流互动。同时，微信公众号会不定期发布有关"彩虹桥"的出版信息，以及汉语阅读、中国文化小知识等。

韩　颖　刘小琳

Preface

For students who study Chinese as a foreign language, it's crucial for them to enlarge the scope of their reading to improve their comprehension skills. The "Rainbow Bridge" Graded Chinese Reader series is designed to provide a collection of interesting and useful Chinese reading materials. This series grades each volume by its vocabulary level and brings the learners into every scene through vivid storytelling. The series has the following features:

I. A gradual approach by grading the volumes based on vocabulary levels. We have consulted the New HSK Vocabulary (2012 Revised Edition), the *Graded Chinese Syllables, Characters and Words for the Application of Teaching Chinese to the Speakers of Other Languages (National Standard)* and the 1,500 Commonly Used High Frequency Chinese Vocabulary, along with the Common European Framework of Reference for Languages (CEFR) to design the "Rainbow Bridge" vocabulary grading standard. The series is divided into seven levels (Starter*, Level 1, Level 2, Level 3, Level 4, Level 5 and Level 6) for students at different stages in their Chinese education to choose from. For each level, new words are no more than 20% of the vocabulary amount as specified in the corresponding HSK and CEFR levels. As the levels progress, the passage length will in turn increase. The following table indicates the corresponding "Rainbow Bridge" level, HSK and CEFR levels, the vocabulary amount, and number of characters.

---

* Represented by "S" on the back cover.

Level	Starter	1	2	3	4	5	6
HSK/ CEFR Level	HSK1 CEFR A1	HSK1-2 CEFR A1-A2	HSK2-3 CEFR A2-B1	HSK3 CEFR A2-B1	HSK3-4 CEFR B1	HSK4 CEFR B1-B2	HSK5 CEFR B2-C1
Vocabulary	150	300	500	750	1,000	1,500	2,500
Characters	1,000	2,500	5,000	7,500	10,000	15,000	25,000

II. Intriguing stories on various themes. The series features engaging stories known for their twists and turns as well as deeply touching plots. The readers will find it a joyful experience to read the stories. The topics are selected from Chinese mythology, legends, folklore, literary classics, biographies of renowned people and historical tales. Such wide-ranging topics exert an invisible, yet formative, influence on readers' understanding of Chinese culture and history.

III. Reasonably structured and easy to use. For each volume of the "Rainbow Bridge" series, apart from a Chinese story, we also provide an introduction to the main characters in Chinese and English, new words with English explanations and sample sentences, and an English translation of the story, followed by comprehension exercises and a vocabulary list to help users read and understand the story and improve their Chinese reading skills. The exercises are mainly presented as objective questions that take on various forms with moderate difficulty. Moreover, keys to the exercises are also provided. The series can be used by teachers in class or by students for self-study.

If you have any questions, comments or suggestions about the series, please email us at liuxiaolin@sinolingua.com.cn. You can also exchange ideas with us via our WeChat account: CHQRainbowBridge. This account will provide updates on the series along with Chinese reading materials and cultural tips.

Han Ying and Liu Xiaolin

中文故事

成也萧何，败也萧何 ①

秦朝末年，社会② 很黑暗③。很多人都想推翻④ 秦朝，建立⑤ 自己的国家。

① 成也萧何，败也萧何（chéngyěxiāohé, bàiyěxiāohé）Success is due to Xiao He, downfall is also due to Xiao He — Success and failure are both attributed to the same person.
韩信因为萧何出名，又因为萧何被杀，真是成也萧何，败也萧何。
② 社会（shèhuì）n. society
e.g., 我希望社会安定。
③ 黑暗（hēi'àn）adj. dark, decadent
e.g., 清朝末年的统治很黑暗。
④ 推翻（tuīfān）v. overthrow
e.g., 人民推翻了国王的统治。
⑤ 建立（jiànlì）v. establish
e.g., 秦始皇建立了秦朝。

有一个叫韩信(Hán Xìn)的人,他很会打仗①。他希望②能被人重用③,建功立业④。

① 打仗(dǎzhàng) v.
fight a war
e.g., 打仗会死很多人。
② 希望(xīwàng) v.
hope
e.g., 我希望人们不要打仗。
③ 重用(zhòngyòng) v.
put sb. in an important position
e.g., 小王受到了老板的重用。
④ 建功立业(jiàngōng-lìyè)
make great contributions and accomplish tasks
e.g., 这个士兵希望能为国家建功立业。

① 军队（jūnduì）n.
troop, army
e.g., 军队担负着保卫国家的任务。

人们都说，<u>汉王 Hànwáng 刘邦 Liú Bāng</u>很了不起。韩信就去了刘邦的<u>军队</u>①。

可是,<u>刘邦只给了韩信一个小官职</u>①,没有重用他。

① 官职(guānzhí)n. official position
e.g., 他的官职不高,权力不大。

① 丞相（chéngxiàng）n. counselor-in-chief
e.g., 国王很信任他的丞相。
② 聪明（cōngmíng）adj. clever
e.g., 我的弟弟很聪明。
③ 聊天（liáotiān）v. chat with
e.g., 我喜欢和爷爷聊天。
④ 才华（cáihuá）n. talent, flair
e.g., 这位年轻的诗人才华横溢，写了很多好作品。
⑤ 向（xiàng）prep. to, towards
e.g., 他做得很对，我们要向他学习。
⑥ 推荐（tuījiàn）v. recommend
e.g., 我想找人帮我，他向我推荐了他的朋友。

刘邦的丞相①萧何是一个很聪明②的人。他和韩信聊天③的时候，知道了韩信很有才华④，就向⑤刘邦推荐⑥韩信。

可是刘邦身边有聪明的萧何、能干的张良，他哪里看得上小小的韩信呢①？

① 呢（ne）aux.
（marker of a special, alternative or rhetorical question）
e.g., 你只是空想，却不去实践，怎么能行呢?

① 逃 (táo) *v.*
escape, flee
e.g., 敌人打不过我们的军队,逃走了。

一天又一天过去了。韩信在刘邦的军队里等了又等,还是没有得到刘邦的重用。他觉得没有希望,就在一个晚上逃① 走了。

萧何知道韩信逃走了，来不及①跟②刘邦说，就骑上马③去追④韩信。

① 来不及（láibùjí）v. not have enough time to do sth.
e.g., 太晚了，来不及去吃饭了。
② 跟（gēn）prep. with, to
e.g., 他跟我说了他的想法，我觉得很好。
③ 骑马（qí mǎ）v. ride a horse
e.g., 我不会骑马。
④ 追（zhuī）v. chase, run after
e.g., 他跑得很快，你追不上他。

① 吧（ba）aux. (used at the end of an imperative sentence to soften the tone)
e.g., 明天你跟我一起去买东西吧。

萧何追了两天，才追上韩信。他对韩信说："汉王很了不起，他一定能成就大事业。请你跟我回去，我们一起帮他吧①。"

韩信说:"我也知道汉王很了不起,可是他看不起我,我在他的军队里又有什么用?"

① 感动（gǎndòng）
v. move
e.g., 她被感动得哭了。

萧何说："这一次，我一定好好向汉王推荐你，他一定会重用你的。请跟我回去吧！"韩信被萧何感动①了，他跟着萧何又回到了刘邦的军队。

刘邦听说萧何两天前离开①了军队,觉得他一定是逃走了,非常生气。

① 离开(líkāi)v. leave
e.g., 她很小的时候就离开了家。

可是，没过多久，萧何又来见刘邦了。

刘邦生气地问萧何："你不是逃走了吗，又回来做什么？"

<u>萧何</u>说:"我不是要逃走,我是去追一个逃走的人。"

刘邦看看萧何,说:"我们的军队里逃走的人很多,你都没有去追过。这一次逃走的人是谁?你为什么要去追?"

① 本事（běnshi）n. ability, capability e.g., 你有本事就不要找人帮你。

萧何笑了笑，说："以前那些逃走的人没什么本事①，走就走了。这次走的人可是能帮你成就大事的韩信，我一定要追！"

萧何这么重视①韩信，让刘邦终于知道，韩信真的是难得的人才。他说："我没有重用韩信，他一定很生气，怎么办②呢？"

① 重视（zhòngshì）v. pay attention to
e.g., 老师很重视大家的意见。
② 怎么办（zěnmebàn）what shall we do
e.g., 我不知道应该怎么办，你知道吗?

萧何笑着说:"韩信是要做大事的人,小官他是看不上的。叫他做大将军,他就不会生气了。"刘邦想了想,同意了。

韩信成了大将军,用自己的本事帮刘邦打仗,建立了很多功业。刘邦做了皇帝①以后,韩信也成了王②。

① 皇帝(huángdì) n. emperor
e.g., 这个皇帝非常年轻。
② 王(wáng) n. king
e.g., 古时候,皇帝的兄弟一般都会当王。

① 皇后（huánghòu）
n. empress
e.g., 皇后是皇帝的妻子。

后来，韩信想推翻刘邦，自己当皇帝。刘邦的妻子吕皇后①知道了，就问萧何应该怎么办。

萧何想了想，说："我们就说皇帝要请韩信到皇宫①来吃饭，他进宫以后，我们就把他抓②起来。"就这样，韩信一进皇宫，就被吕皇后抓住杀死了。

① 皇宫（huánggōng）
n. imperial palace
e.g., 皇帝住在皇宫里。
② 抓（zhuā）v.
arrest, catch
e.g., 小偷被大家一起抓住了。

① 同样（tóngyàng）
adv. similarly, likewise
e.g., 妈妈爱孩子，同样，孩子也很爱妈妈。

因为萧何的推荐，韩信才得到了重用；同样①，也是因为萧何，韩信不但没有推翻汉朝，还被杀死了。

韩信的成功①和失败②都跟萧何有关系③。有时候，朋友和敌人④的转变⑤真的很奇妙⑥——这就是中国人说的"成也萧何，败也萧何"。

① 成功（chénggōng）
n. success
e.g., 有自己的事业才是成功吗？我觉得不是。
② 失败（shībài）n. failure
e.g., 他不能忍受自己的失败。
③ 关系（guānxi）v. be related to
e.g., 这是他的想法，和我没有关系。
④ 敌人（dírén）n. enemy
e.g., 你的敌人就是你自己。
⑤ 转变（zhuǎnbiàn）v. convert
e.g., 有时候，朋友会转变成敌人，敌人也有可能转变成朋友。
⑥ 奇妙（qímiào）
adj. marvelous, miraculous
e.g., 他们的关系很奇妙，是朋友，也是敌人。

English Version

Xiao He: A Blessing and a Curse

The end of the Qin Dynasty (221 BC-206 BC) was a time of tuormoil Many people wanted to overthrow Qin and establish a new country.

There was a man at that time named Han Xin who was a skilled military strategist and tactician. He hoped to be put in a key position to achieve great success.

It was said that Liu Bang, King of the Han, was quite capable, so Han Xin went to join Liu's army.

However, Liu Bang offered him the role of a minor official instead of a post with high stature.

Xiao He, counselor-in-chief of Liu Bang, was quite a wise person. When chatting with Han Xin, Xiao found him resourceful and recommended him to Liu Bang.

But Liu Bang already had two loyal assistants: the smart Xiao He and the capable Zhang Liang. What would make him take notice of Han Xin, such a small figure?

While serving in Liu's army, Han Xin waited day by day to be promoted to a more important position. As time passed and the opportunity never presented itself, he fell into despair. One night he fled the army.

After hearing that Han Xin had fled, Xiao He immediately set out to chase him on horseback without wasting time to report to the king.

It took Xiao He two days to catch up with Han Xin. He told Han Xin, "The King of the Han is an extraordinary person. He is bound to achieve great accomplishments. Please come back with me. Together we can help him."

Han Xin said, "I know the King of the Han is quite competent, but he looks down on me. What is the point of me continuing to serve in his army?"

Xiao He said, "This time, I will make a strong recommendation to the King, and he will surely promoto you to a key position. Let's return together." Han Xin was moved by Xiao He's words, so he rejoined Liu's army following Xiao He.

When Liu Bang was told that Xiao He had left the army two days earlier, he flew into a rage, believing that Xiao must have deserted him.

However, Xiao came back after a short while.

Liu Bang asked Xiao He in a fury, "What's the point of coming back after you fled?"

Xiao He replied, "I am not a deserter. I went to chase the one who fled."

Glancing at Xiao He, Liu Bang said, "Many in the army have fled, but you never chased them before. Who is the deserter? Why did you give chase this time?"

Xiao He said with a smile, "All those escapees were ordinary people, so if they wanted to leave, I let them go. But this person,

Han Xin, can aid you in achieving great success, so I had to give chase."

Xiao He's high regard for Han xin finatly made Liu Bang realize that Han Xin was a person of high caliber. "Han Xin must have been furious that I had not put him in a key position," he said. "What should I do?"

Xiao He said with a smile, "Han Xin had high hopes for great success, so the title of a minor official didn't match his ambition. But if you appoint him general-in-chief, he won't be angry anymore." Liu Bang followed Xiao He's advice after thinking for a while.

After Han Xin became general-in-chief, he helped Liu Bang to victory in war, achieving great success. Liu Bang then became the emperor and conferred the title of the king on Han Xin.

Later, Han Xin tried to usurp the throne. As soon as Empress Lü, Liu Bang's wife, heard the news, she asked Xiao He what they should do.

Xiao He thought for a while and said, "We can tell Han Xin that the emperor wants to invite him to a dinner. Once he enters the palace, we can arrest him." As planned, they caught Han Xin and killed him.

Thanks to Xiao He's recommendation, Han Xin was given an important position. Meanwhile, because of Xiao He, Han Xin failed in overthrowing the Han and was executed instead.

Han Xin's success and failure were both due to Xiao He. The transformation from friends to foes is sometimes miraculous. This story thus gives rise to the said idiom.

课前练习 Warm-up exercises

一、朗读下面的词语。Read the following phrases.

chéng yě xiāo hé, bài yě xiāo hé　　tuīfān Qíncháo
成也萧何，败也萧何　　推翻秦朝

tuīfān Liú Bāng　　jiànlì guójiā　　chéngjiù shìyè
推翻刘邦　　建立国家　　成就事业

二、思考题。Pre-reading questions.

1. 萧何为什么先是帮助韩信，后来又帮吕皇后杀了他？

2. 你觉得萧何和韩信到底是什么关系？

课后练习 Reading exercises

一、按照故事内容排列顺序。Put the following statements in order according to the story.

1. 萧何向刘邦推荐韩信
2. 萧何去追韩信
3. 萧何帮吕皇后杀死韩信
4. 刘邦重用韩信
5. 韩信去刘邦的军队
6. 韩信逃离刘邦的军队
7. 刘邦当上皇帝

正确的顺序是：_____

二、为下列各题选择正确的答案。Choose the correct answer according to the story.

1. 韩信去刘邦的军队是因为（　　）。

   A. 刘邦会重用他　　　B. 刘邦会让他当个小官
   C. 他希望成就大事业　D. 他想当皇帝

2. 谁知道韩信是一个有真本事的人？（　　）

   A. 刘邦　　　B. 萧何
   C. 张良　　　D. 没有人

3. 军队里逃走的人很多，萧何为什么只去追韩信？（　　）

　　A. 只有韩信是他的朋友　　B. 韩信是他的敌人

　　C. 刘邦喜欢韩信　　　　　D. 韩信是有真本事的人

4. 萧何为什么帮吕皇后杀死韩信？（　　）

　　A. 萧何不喜欢韩信　　　　B. 韩信不喜欢萧何

　　C. 韩信想当皇帝　　　　　D. 萧何想当皇帝

5. "成也萧何，败也萧何"是什么意思？（　　）

　　A. 成为萧何和打败萧何

　　B. 萧何也成功了，也失败了

　　C. 成功了没什么了不起，失败了也没关系

　　D. 朋友和敌人的转变很奇妙

三、判断题：请根据故事内容判断下列说法是否正确，如果正确请标"T"，不正确请标"F"。
Decide whether the following statements are true (T) or false (F).

1. 韩信刚去刘邦的军队，就得到了重用。（　　）

2. 张良向刘邦推荐了韩信。（　　）

3. 韩信没有得到重用，就逃走了。（　　）

4. 知道韩信逃走了，萧何骑着马去追他。（　　）

5. 韩信想当皇帝，被刘邦抓住杀死了。（　　）

四、看图复述故事内容。Fill in the blanks to retell the story using the pictures.

1. 有一个叫韩信的人，很会打仗。他希望能_____人_____，建功立业。

2. 萧何和韩信聊天的时候，知道了韩信很有才华，就_____刘邦_____韩信。

3. 萧何知道韩信逃走了，_____跟刘邦说，就骑上马去追韩信。

4. 后来，韩信想推翻刘邦，自己当皇帝。刘邦的妻子吕皇后知道了，就问萧何应该_____。

5.韩信的成功和失败都_____萧何_____。有时候,朋友和敌人的转变真的很奇妙——这就是中国人说的"成也萧何,败也萧何"。

课后练习题答案 Keys to the exercises

一、按照故事内容排列顺序
5—1—6—2—4—7—3

二、为下列各题选择正确的答案
1. C　　2. B　　3. D　　4. C　　5. D

三、判断题：请根据故事内容判断下列说法是否正确，如果正确请标"T"，不正确请标"F"
1. F　　2. F　　3. T　　4. T　　5. F

四、看图复述故事内容
1. 被　重用
2. 向　推荐
3. 来不及
4. 怎么办
5. 和　有关系

词汇表
Vocabulary List

吧	aux.	ba	(used at the end of an imperative sentence to soften the tone)
本事	n.	běnshi	ability, capability
才华	n.	cáihuá	talent, flair
成功	n.	chénggōng	success
丞相	n.	chéngxiàng	counselor-in-chief
成也萧何，败也萧何		chéngyěxiāohé, bàiyěxiāohé	Success is due to Xiao He, downfall is also due to Xiao He — Success and failure are both attributed to the same person.
聪明	adj.	cōngmíng	clever
打仗	v.	dǎzhàng	fight a war
敌人	n.	dírén	enemy
感动	v.	gǎndòng	move
跟	prep.	gēn	with, to
关系	v.	guānxi	be related to
官职	n.	guānzhí	official position
黑暗	adj.	hēi'àn	dark, decadent
皇帝	n.	huángdì	emperor
皇宫	n.	huánggōng	imperial palace
皇后	n.	huánghòu	empress
建功立业		jiàngōng-lìyè	make great contributions and accomplish tasks
建立	v.	jiànlì	establish
军队	n.	jūnduì	troop, army
来不及	v.	láibùjí	not have enough time to do sth.
聊天	v.	liáotiān	chat with
离开	v.	líkāi	leave
呢	aux.	ne	(marker of a special, alternative or rhetorical question)
骑马	v.	qí mǎ	ride a horse

奇妙	adj.	qímiào	marvelous, miraculous
社会	v.	shèhuì	society
失败	n.	shībài	failure
逃	v.	táo	escape, flee
同样	adv.	tóngyàng	similarly, likewise
推翻	v.	tuīfān	overthrow
推荐	v.	tuījiàn	recommend
王	n.	wáng	king
向	prep.	xiàng	to, towards
希望	v.	xīwàng	hope
怎么办		zěnmebàn	what shall we do
重视	v.	zhòngshì	pay attention to
重用	v.	zhòngyòng	put sb. in an important position
抓	v.	zhuā	arrest, catch
转变	v.	zhuǎnbiàn	convert
追	v.	zhuī	chase, run after

项目策划：韩　颖　刘小琳
责任编辑：韩　颖
英文编辑：范逊敏
英文审定：黄长奇　James Hutchison
插图绘制：赵倩倩
设计指导：战文庭　卞　淳
设计制作：isles studio

图书在版编目（CIP）数据

成也萧何，败也萧何 / 叶婵娟改编. -- 北京：华语教学出版社，2018.1
（"彩虹桥"汉语分级读物. 入门级：150 词）
ISBN 978-7-5138-1479-9

Ⅰ. ①成… Ⅱ. ①叶… Ⅲ. ①汉语－对外汉语教学－语言读物　Ⅳ. ① H195.5

中国版本图书馆 CIP 数据核字（2017）第 313330 号

成也萧何，败也萧何

叶婵娟　改编
吴爱俊　翻译

＊

©华语教学出版社有限责任公司
华语教学出版社有限责任公司出版
（中国北京百万庄大街24号　邮政编码 100037）
电话：(86)10-68320585　68997826
传真：(86)10-68997826　68326333
网址：www.sinolingua.com.cn
电子信箱：hyjx@sinolingua.com.cn
北京京华虎彩印刷有限公司印刷
2018年（32开）第1版
2018年第1版第1次印刷
（汉英）
ISBN 978-7-5138-1479-9
定价：15.00元